AF455182

Chimeric Machines

by Lucy A. Snyder

Chimeric Machines
by Lucy A. Snyder

Creative Guy Publishing
Vancouver British Columbia Canada

Trade paperback edition
ISBN-10 1-894953-55-X
ISBN-13 978-1-894953-55-9
First Printing March 2009

www.creativeguypublishing.com

Chimeric Machines

by Lucy A. Snyder

Creative Guy Publishing
Vancouver | Canada

Contents

Part V Daughters of Typhon

Part VI Strange Corners

Part VII Unshelled Evolution

Chi*mer"ic a. [Gr. a she-goat, a chimera]

Imaginary; fanciful; fantastic. Of or relating to a chimera, a monster represented as vomiting flames, and as having the head of a lion, the body of a goat, and the tail of a dragon.

Ma*chine" n. [F., fr. L. *machina* machine, engine, device, trick, Gr., from means, expedient.]

1. In general, any combination of bodies so connected that their relative motions are constrained, and by means of which force and motion may be transmitted and modified.
2. Any mechanical contrivance, as the wooden horse with which the Greeks entered Troy.
3. A person who acts at the will of another.
4. A combination of persons acting together for a common purpose, with the agencies that they use; as, the social machine.
5. Supernatural agency in a poem.

Taken from: *Webster's Dictionary*, 1913.

for Gary

Introduction

by Tom Piccirilli

Okay, so you've picked up this collection, which already proves that you're sharper than the kid you sat behind in Homeroom who used to spit in his textbooks, your step-brother George who used to call you "bookworm" and thumb your glasses, and the automotive shop teacher who caught you with *Leaves of Grass* in the tenth grade and told you that poetry is just "namby-pamby rhymes about rocks and rivers."

You, pal, have a head on your shoulders, and you're eager to dip deeply into Lucy Snyder's verse and prose poems. You've laid out your hard-earned cash and you're expecting good things. And I'm here to tell you that it was a smart move on your part because you're about to receive. You surely are.

Let me show you what I'm talking about. Perk up in your LA-Z-BOY for a second and just listen to this for a title: "And There in the Machine, Virginia Finally Stood Up." Now, is that a hook or is that a hook? It's impossible for anybody with two functioning brain synapses not to immediately have their imagination fired up the moment your eyes rest on those words. Snyder knows that the first hurdle between a writer and reader is the title. It's not the first scene or the first paragraph or even the first sentence. It's the title, and she's going to grab you by the guts early.

And if there's the faintest echo of that auto shop teacher or your goddamn brother George still wafting around at the back your skull telling you that maybe you've stumbled upon a Susan Polis Schultz wannabe, and you're worried that those rhyming couplets are going to sneak out from behind the next page, then check out these pitch-perfect, hammer-hard lines from "Subtlety":

> Subtlety came to us from Latin
> (by way of the clever French)
> in that thin, gossamer term
> subtilis, which in turn
> is a web of under-stitched
> subtext. What joe really gives
>
> a flying doublefudge fuck
> about lacy coy underwords?

Go ahead and read it again. I'll wait.

All set?

Snyder's work is complex yet grounded. You can read it on several levels and it'll work on each and every one. It's lyrical but rooted in authenticity and validity. There's truth here, and tackling the truth is the highest calling of any poet.

So many amazing lines just leap out at the reader, like this one from "After the Funeral": *Mom's a brick of ash in a Baptist wall/and the nest I made stayed empty.*

Doesn't that slip a knife between your ribs and

tickle your heart?

That's the effect of a hard-fought gospel. Lucy Snyder has seen some shit, brother. She's been through the trenches; she knows the way the world comes down. You can feel it in the work. You're not just looking at words in a book, you're regarding a life that's been opened up and splashed down on the page. You think that's easy? This lady is not only courageous, she's fearless. We need more like her to give us that grand plucking of the guts.

So be brave, Chuckles, and be ready.

Because you're about to be disturbed, fascinated, entranced and bruised. Now thank your lucky stars and move on to what awaits....

Part I
Technica

Modernism

The statuesque dove lay perfect
in Old World gray and white
folded pinions parallel
head perpendicular
a classic sight.

A meter above the dove
on the plate glass where
the bird had mistaken open air
was an abstract slanted splash
of translucent crimson.

And There in the Machine, Virginia Finally Stood Up

Class, settle down, get out your textbooks, and turn to page 43. After we're done reading, we can have show-and-tell for thirty minutes. No, Virginia, you can't go first – we'll go in alphabetical order like always. Sit down, Virginia; you can tell us about your trip when it's your turn. I'm sorry we ran out of time before we got to you last month, but you still have to wait your turn. Now, everyone: turn to page 43.

You're a good player, Virginia, but Joseph is two grades ahead of you. He's had private lessons, and he's got a much better instrument. It's his turn to be first chair. You have to blend with his sound; don't draw attention to yourself.

Oh, Ginny, you're not going to wear *that* dress to the party, are you? It's far too loud; don't you want to wear your nice pink one instead? You don't want the boys to get the wrong idea, do you? Now, remember, you mustn't be too forward; if a boy wants to dance with you, he'll ask. Don't talk too much. Remember to smile. Boys like girls who smile.

He's out of your league, Gin. You're no cheerleader. No, you shouldn't even try to talk to him. Just hang out with us at the dance; we're your *real* friends. He's out of your league.

Hey, Gin, why are you wasting your time in front of that old typewriter? Come to the party with us! You don't want to be a nerd, do you?

Ginny, I'm really proud that you got into MIT, but we just can't afford it now that your father's retired. I'm sorry, honey, but the scholarship just isn't big enough. I know we sent your brother, but that's different. He's going to be an engineer; you just want to major in English, right? Boston is so far away, and big cities are terribly dangerous. Now, honey, be reasonable! The local college is perfectly decent. That's better. I knew we could count on you to be a good girl.

Ms. Wilson, you did a very nice job in fiction class, so your "A" was well-deserved. What? No, I'm afraid I can't let you take my upper-level workshop. Yes, I know there's a seat left, but I simply can't allow non-MFAs into my workshop. The undergraduate program is one thing, but our graduate school is *quite* exclusive. We prefer students who are not local. Your fiction is very competent, but I doubt you could compete with writers from larger schools.

Miss Wilson, I realize you've been working here longer than Mr. Jones, but he's got a degree from Harvard and a family to support. He's got the go-getter attitude that we want to see in our managers. I understand your frustration, but I can't promote every deserving employee. Be a good team player; we might be able to find a secretarial position for you in a year or two.

Hey, Gin, what's up? Haven't seen you in years. What? You wrote a book? Oh. That's cool, I guess. I could write one too, you know. If I *wanted*. Been working on my golf game, you know? Golf's *hard*.

Miss Wilson, I'd appreciate it if you didn't have your book cover on display in your cubicle. It's not conducive to a productive work environment. Yes, I know the others have football and Nascar posters up, but sports are ... normal. Some of the others think you're ... overstepping yourself. After all, anyone can self-publish ... what? You mean someone *paid* you to write that? Who on Earth would want to read a book written by a *secretary*? Well, then, the cover's a commercial. Employees are forbidden to use company resources for personal gain. The cube wall is a company resource. Take the cover down.

Miss Wilson?

What's that in your hand?

Subtlety

Subtlety came to us from Latin
(by way of the clever French)
in that thin, gossamer term
subtilis, which in turn
is a web of under-stitched
subtext. What joe really gives

a flying doublefudge fuck
about lacy coy underwords?
Twixt the stark, sooty verbs
it's card tricks in a tar-dark hall,
earnest *Kama Sutra* recitations
to a rubber smutstore doll.

A horse is a horse unless
she's a Mississippi queen, an allegory
crawling from a swamp of contempt.
I metaphor lunch, but the queen
wouldn't listen, baffled by menus
plain as her face. Moot.
Mute. Mote. Moat.
The meanings collapse,
drown in that lazy river.
Undercurrents churn mud.

Sympathy

Sympathy evolved peripherally,
a selective way to keep the tribe alive
through the secondhand pangs of trial,
tributaries of tribulation shared by blood,
our hardwired love of Rover and Fluffy just
a shadow of family need in the genes.

But what if we could feel the flesh we eat,
taste the fatal throes ol' Bossie endured
as the butcher put a hammer to her head?
What if every whitemeat nugget sliding
greasy down our throats held a grindhouse
flash of Chicken Little, debeaked and choked?

Would we shun personalized burgers
and embrace plates of cheerful fruits?
Would we eagerly flee from carnivory,
ban the slaughter and celebrate salad,
glorify veggies, their tales of pain so dull;
no yardman names the blades he mows.

But righteous sadists might dictate diets of woe:
priests would curse the sins in mother's milk
and tell their flocks to feed the babies Bambi.
Hardening souls for a Heavenly shine, pious
soldiers would savor Apocalyptic glory
in the soylent flesh of every blessed enemy.

Trepanation

The first migraine-plagued caveman
who countered his aching cranium
with crudely pounded flint (and lived)
surely shared his medical breakthrough.

Headcutting is old as woodcutting.
Andean shaman or Alpine physician,
a good doctor knew the value
of airing out a fevered brain.

In dark ages before Lister and Pasteur,
chirurgeons didn't know a virus
from a curse, but they needed a name
for the rusty saw they used to open
a blow-swelled skull: the trepane
saved careless patricians from coma.

Modern surgeons' steel is clean, but treat
tyro trepanation with trepidation. Teen
mystics sing high of tuning third eyes
and praise their cordless doorknob drills
for opening new windows of perception
even as they lie blinded, bacterial feasts.

Tech Support

We sit at gray monitors, listening
to confused Eloi in tusky towers
divergently evolving. Always
there's a compatibility problem
between the overfocused poets
and the language of machines.

The Eloi cry doom over bright wires,
voices spores. Our minds fuzz mycotic.
No dystopia's perfect: we have a bitter savior
so we shamble, spidery, pale, seeking ambrosia.
Faith's no narcotic once you've lost humanity,
so we take noon communion in free hot coffee.

The Fish and the Bicycle

Consider the physics:
how could she pedal
with fragile membranous fins,
sit with slippery tail,
steer with gasping mouth?

She breaks the surface,
peeks up goggle-eyed
at his bold chrome frame,
his knobby cocked handlebar,
his rugged hunky tires.

Dory knows that Schwinns can't swim.
Undersea, the salt and wet
would rot his shapely seat,
rust his shining chain,
blister his pearly paint.

But she'd be happy to drown in the air,
flip and flop on the gritty boardwalk,
shake to flakes in the stinking heat
for just a single slimy ride
on her Adonis machine.

Part II
Quiet Places

glowfish

they say that fancy angelfish
glow brightest right before
they die. I never had an angel
just a mother
and she glowed so bright
the sun fled my sky

hired guns in white coats
can't slay the knight
on his ivory horse
but they'll boast
they know the cold odds
and bet you a warm future

tired nurses
hang futile silver bags
as the crab devours my mother
I hold her close
and memorize the lines
in her palms

the Moirae weave
a tricky double-helix
genes don't lie
but they can hide
more spiders
than Arachne's closet

in my empty home I scrub
her blood from my clothes
when the sun finally comes
I find her shade
in every photograph
and mirror

But. I know I must
look to my own hand
to unravel the strands

dwelling in the webs
inside your own head
makes for a crabbed life
better to be a fish and swim
as hard as you can to the sun
and glow

After the Funeral

Buttery adagio light drips through
the berry-heavy pyracantha branches
where cardinals cautiously feast, their soft
chit-chit-chit of alarm a siren song
to Uno, stalking beneath, keenly unaware
that his albino fur flashes his presence
to the tasty twittermeats that pivot,
plié and flit from twig to fruit,
a scrumpy rumba for any feline.

Last year, I'd let him have his fun,
but Mom wept over every cracked egg;
I call him away from precious nestlings.
His prim savagery will be soothed
if I let him lick my ice cream spoon:
butter pecan from Gandy's Dairy.
He'll flee if I play Mom's Verdi; *E l'amore*
lo lusinghi must be some kitty obscenity,
the opposite of Momma's plain lullabies
as she rocked me asleep on the veranda
in the warm honeysuckle breezes.

Mom's a brick of ash in a Baptist wall
and the nest I made stayed empty;
Uno's happy to play the changeling,
curled, purring while I rock him in my lap
as the sun sinks in the red-feathered sky.

Mute Birth

The green country sawbones
called it mute birth: the blue-
faced babes with bad hearts
couldn't give a healthy cry.
No cure, almost no science
applied to distinguish
the doomed from those
choking. And so

my newborn father was set aside
as a lost cause beyond young
hemorrhaging grandmother,
his faint cardiac flutter,
oxygen fading in his veins,
skin pasty, then purpling
dark as slate pavestones
slicked with winter rain.

But the old nurse noticed
his chest's fitful rise and fall,
got the bellows in his throat,
cleared the suffocating clots
and his heart. Was fine.
Was fine. His heart. Was fine.

Home For The Holidays

Six months past the New Year's
car crash, I heard him from beyond
the grave: "Honey, I'll be with you
in time for Christmas." And my love

was true. Elms blushed for autumn
when his appendix arrived,
pink as Labor Day sunburn.
How our baby laughed to see it!

Then his pumpkin-fat spleen,
just in time for Halloween.
Icy Thanksgiving roads
glazed in warm vodka

served up his steady legs.
The last chilly Chanukah night
his sweet Manischewitz toast
brought the rest of him home.

Our family will share
the Yuletide snug
in our dark pine abode
beneath December snows.

Worm and Memory

It'd be nice to flourish
a wand in clever magic,
gracefully draw a caustic
gray thread from the head
and drop it, splashless,
in a cool gazing pool.

We cerebrated monkeys
seldom find any witchy
pennies for our thoughts;
our long-tailed guilts,
shames and rages grow
like *Dracunculus* worms:
burning, blistering, itchy.

Milky little demons are best
twisted out in private, a bit
at a time; in the healthy light
the worms can spin to gold.

Part III
Dark Dreams

Babel's Children
for JN Williamson

From the paperback cover
twin boys stare, smugly
grinning in generic blue

polo shirts, sandy Seventies
bowl haircuts. Squinty eyes,
the kind of smarmy brats

the author wanted to kick
in grade school. His kid
protagonists weren't punks.

The artist sweated sudden deadlines
under the publisher's leaden budget.
Everyone owed a holy mortgage, so

the author lived with what he got.
The cover twins resembled
the author's own sons: flunked

freshman English, grew sullen
mullets and forgot their father
after they found God.

When the author died, his frail
neighbors arranged a memorial
in the nursing home cafeteria.

The sour sons arrived alongside
a glycerine-weeping preacher
in a blue Swaggart suit.

He hijacked the shabby service,
denounced the dead man's books,
tried to hellfire some scratch

out of the stoic dying mourners,
spun snaky webs twixt the kinless
roots of "penthouse" and "repent"

as if dodging godless sin was just
to win an afterlife-raffled mansion.
The boys gifted the preacher 20 bucks,

scoured their dad's tiny room for prizes.
Found his adored *Penthouse* collection,
burned the dogeared stash in a pious

blacktop barbecue. Piled their pop's
life works in brown paper bags
and dropped them for pennies

at a handy Half-Price Books.
The clerk, who was perked
to find a signed first edition,

set the blueshirt kids to smirk
at shoppers from behind locked glass.

Meanwhile, a drunk crematory stiff
dumped the author's unclaimed ash.

Beggars' Night
co-written with Gary A. Braunbeck

Stinky kid sneakers peek beneath
ghostly sheets and shredded zombie jeans.
Chatty moms herd sugarbuzzed superheroes
and tween princesses off strangers' lawns
onto frosty concrete to await safe treats.

But half past nine, flashlight batteries die,
buzzing streetlamps flicker to silent black
as scudding clouds blot the gibbous moon;
manly hearts jump as small sweaty fingers
impatiently twist free from daddies' hands.

And in the sudden dark, for just a moment,
cheap cotton gauze spins to Egyptian linen,
latex and greasepaint become twitching scars,
hairy feral muscle splits wispy nylon rags,
and every smile stinks of clotted blood.

But in a heartbeat, the dire clouds retreat,
the moon shines brave and the lamps relight.
Trembling parents retrieve little tricksters,
ruffle hair, press hands to narrow chests,
unable to feel the monsters burning inside.

Prometheus

My pain's become an impure joy;
I wait for you on this windswept rock,
the granite and iron hard against my flesh.
My blood quickens when I hear your call.

Tear into me, my love.
Draw a talon across my shivering skin,
lick the blood from my spreading wounds,
let me feel the sweet agony of your bite.

Let me be your Adam.
Yank a rib from my trembling flank
and pleasure yourself upon it
until my ears ring with your ecstasy.

Rip apart my sweating flesh,
devour me in greedy beakfuls.
Flay me, crush me, love me
'til the stones hide their faces.

The Monster between The Sparks

I am the death you cannot see
when you gaze upon your starry skies.
Your telescopes, they lie to you
when they show a cosmos glittering
with a million fiery gems;
I lurk unseen between those sparks,
swelling, growing larger and smarter
with every sun I swallow whole.

I've grown tired of passive fare;
worlds and stars and dust,
all spiral to my maw
with no effort, just the force
of my immense dark gravity. I want
prey that thinks itself a predator,
a victim that will find its way to me
carried on the silver wings of mortal pride,
prey that fights and feels the terror of my bite.

I know you'll fly to me; babies can't resist
the shiny, pretty things, reaching for a bauble
lying near the snake, grasping at the flame
that burns soft flesh. You'll try for worlds
to replace the one you broke
and when you come I'll crush you
to my frozen breast and take you to my heart
of darkness, and your pain will keep me warm.

I am the death you cannot see,
I am all you cannot bear
to know about your universe,
because to know that I am real
is to know there's no escape
from this, your fragile world,
your tiny azure ember burning down
in the cold of an endless night.

Part IV
Crete, Kentucky

Passie Fay's Lament

I know it's white-trash as a whole
box of Little Debbies for breakfast,
a baloney sandwich fried in Crisco
because you can't afford real butter,

but I swear to you, I never knew
that boy was growing inside me;
I'd birthed six kids for King;
it didn't feel a thing like before.

I was trying to ditch these hips.
I was buying celery, broccoli
and cabbage on sale at Aldi
so I thought he was just gas.

Ari kept telling me, "Momma,
there's a purdy lady inside you
just waitin' to make a jailbreak
from that fulsome prison of fat."

It sure weren't June Carter come bustin'
out when my water broke all over
the Wal-Mart's restroom floor;
a trucker helped deliver my surprise.

King threw me out of the house that night;
one look at the baby, he knew I'd fucked
Bull White. Lil' Terry favors him so close
it's like Whitey's juice just grew on its own.

Mama warned me not to eat rotten apples,
but King's dick went dead from pills
and booze. Whitey is a brutal fool,
but a gal like me is lucky for anyone's fancy.

My life's leaking through my redneck mistake;
even Ari left me to fend for myself in this maze
with a bullhead boy who laughs while he breaks
my grandma's china and chowhounds our trailer.

Flyboy

The baseheads call me Daddy Luzz like I'm fly.
I was my momma's first, a cream-faced baby boy.
Pops thought I was ace, raised me like a king,
named me for the light of the Las Vegas sun.
Or maybe pale Lucifer. No one would know
to see me now: sun burnt my skin as dark as Coke.

In college, I gene-spliced corn to make cocaine.
With a chemistry book in my hand, I could fly.
I wish I'd made Christian use of what I know,
but like Momma said, "Folly, thy name be Boy."
She hoped I'd be a NASA man blazing past the sun,
but my Supernaut Jiffypop made me campus king.

It's a crackbrain thing to think you're king;
I tossed around cash from frankenstein coke
and party girls loved me like God's risen son.
But I was just a buzzing mosquito, a robber fly
sucking profit from the uptown mobster boys
who lectured me with fists and guns. I knew

to blow to cowtowns where I wasn't known.
Spit-quick, I found hilljack saviors: Mr. King
and Passie Fay made me their moonshine boy,
kept me copsafe while I cropped up their coke.
For a while, life was stingless as a butterfly.
I took a woman, built my manor in the sun.

My wife stroked out giving birth to our son.
When I held bawling Russ, in my gut I knew
it was time to get real, get straight, time to fly.
That wasn't The Man's pharming plan. Ol' King
flared hot as a blast furnace combusting coke
when I asked if I could stop. He said, "Boy,

I'll throw you to the narcs; they'll bury your boy
in the county home while you bust rocks in the sun."
So. I've plotted our route while I plow out the coke.
I found a broken-down turboprop in a barn. I know
more than chemistry and genes: engineering's king.
With parts and practice, my boy and I can fly.

I've got to keep my son safe; I've got to quit this coke.
Russ thinks he'll be Sky King; boy's gotta watch the sun,
fly for the sea, get free of this mazed-up life I've known.

Terror White

I work alone on the snowman's land,
sleep on rags behind a maze of doors.
Coulda been a star like my old man.

When Luzz split, it all hit the fan.
Never saw King hate anyone more.
I work alone on the snowman's land.

King told me I was part of his plan;
he'd never wanted me around before.
Coulda been a star like my old man.

Took my lessons in a windowless van,
learned guns and grams and gore.
I work alone on the snowman's land.

King made me quit school to serve his clan,
told me a quarterback's arm is made for war.
But I coulda been a star like my old man.

When the bitches get into my van,
I do what I want to them and more.
I kill alone on the snowman's land
cuz I shoulda been a star like my old man.

Cissy Cocalus

It ain't right for a girl in my line of work to fall
in love, but I gotta say, that Luzz is some fine
man. He always talkin' 'bout his cute lil' boy,
make me think maybe I'd be happy with a baby
someday. Anyway, he always clean, and tip
real good. Then this guy King come to town,
ready to fuck up Luzz for pure wicked sport.
Luzz give me a triple fee and packets of sweet
laced with dope. Tell me to go to this one motel.
King like to get head in the bath and sip moon;
all I gotta do is fluff him, spike his drink,
draw the tub water and just let him drown.

I sit on the john as his breath blubs away;
murdering makes a damn sexy payday.

Ari, Pushing Forty

Back home, they figure sixteen
is a fine ripe time to drop your first pup
but I tell you: it's a bone dumb age.

I still thought Pa was sweet as Christmas pie.
I still believed the prunefaced TV preachers
when they said human need's some kind of sin;

I shouldn't have turned my back on my own
mama, even if her baby wasn't my Pa's. Who
else was gonna help her? Macho jock Bull? Ha.

Terry was still my brother, my blood, even at the end
when we found all those poor Mexican girls cut up
like fryer hens all over Luzz's abandoned mansion.

Luzz. That man was a piece of work.
When I was twenty-three, he gave me
the keys to Club Cirque and I believed

that he was gonna leave his wife,
take me out dancing every night once
she was done having his son. Dumb.

I'm sorry to say I ain't been much smarter since then.
Ed Shutes? He's a real piece of *something*. I showed him
the way thru the mansion. Easy to lose yourself in there.

Ed swore that he just wanted to talk to Terry
about my daddy's drugs, but I guess finding a mess
of tortured corpses is gonna change any cop's mind.

FBI, DEA ... whatever. A cop's a cop, even if he's got
pretty blue eyes and knows "Freebird" on slide guitar.
He played me all the way from Crete to Daytona Beach,

said he was going out for a cigar and never came back.
I waited forever, got a clue, went down to the hotel well
and told my sad story to Donnie, the bartender. Bar *owner*,

it turned out, and wouldn't you know, three weeks later
he proposed. Sure, he's been a fine husband, good guy,
keeps me in pretty threads and makes a rockin' martini.

Speaking of: my glass is dry, sweetie ... want to go back
to my room for tonic and gin? Donnie's in Hackensack,
and you look like a boy who knows all my favorite sins.

Part V
Daughters of Typhon

Gigantic

The staff of *Woman's Day* wouldn't be so gauche
as to suggest there's a thin woman inside me

screaming for egress. Their sumptuous cover cakes
are to be cooked, but *never* eaten oneself, communion

given by martyred suburban priestess to loving flock
of orderly children and lawn-worshipping husband.

WD's perky pink bullets of diet tips
slay me, but not my inner elegant lady

because she never existed. *Ma*
femme intérieure a faim et grand.

I mean, she's fucking huge, kids.
And she's not just the one, dear.

Sometimes, she's Cass, idly slothing through
slick chick magazines whose airbrushed ideals

are science-fictional commercials, but the weight
of failed femininity grinds her deep into seat

'til there's nothing left of her will but the drive
for endorphic reward, shoveling twinkies sugar high.

Fried thing, I think I love you.
You make everything greasy.

But then Bertha busts on through, 400 pounds
of muscled heterosex rampaging Valkyrie dyke

sergeant-shouting about damnation of consumption,
swinging thick elbows and hairy roller-derby knees

not at the Patriarchy – pricks do as pricks are – but
at the bowtied notion you need more than a cunt,

that a girlish mammal must wax bare as a frog princess,
buy devilish Prada, kiss double-digit lipstick to become

what you always were. That crazy meat-craving Bertha
is so fucking unfashionable. Sheesh. Nobody wants

to give *her* a conjugal visit. Keep the bitch in solitary
even if she won't quit howling in the starving dark.

Internal Combustion

The lady on the exercise show
talks in calories burned
every hour. 413 for tennis
if you don't have a partner;
236 for soothing Tai Chi.

I want to ask her the count
for smashing an electric dryer
on a hairy wet bathroom floor
blindly sobbing and screaming
until your vocal cords crack.

I bend to unplug the sparking remains
as a commercial clatters, dumb company
that tells me nothing about home repair.
The exercise lady glows and smiles,
bends herself into a clever yoga pose:
244 calories and the dog faces down.

At The Rec Center

A homely baby in a school ruled by pretty
young ladies, you wear your lonely puppyfat
to the pool, swimming slow under your Speedo,

nearly twelve, invisible unless it's your turn to be
teased. Every girl turns, sighs: it's handsome Jamey
... he looks right at you, waves and calls your name!

You swim to the edge, smitten. He smiles whitely,
nothing like a shark and says, "I've got something
to show you; wanna come?" You can't wait to see!

You flounder onto concrete and follow behind,
flimsy suit dripping, young soul skipping
with joy that the boy wants to be your friend.

Down the hall in the abandoned handball courts,
it's just yellow flickery lights and gritty sock dust.
The lamps snap out; the slam of the switch echoes,

shocking as your father's shout. Confusion curdling
to terror in the dark, all you can sense is the stink
of stinging chlorine and sweat. Jamey's laughing

and something sticky, something rubbery pokes
into your palm and you bolt to the crack of light
at the door, escape as his mocking calls choke

poisonous and loud as atomic grenades, ashes,
ashes, you want to fall down, blow away but you run
and don't stop 'til you're home to wash yourself raw.

Infinite Loop: Girl with Black Eye

— the kick shocks your brain blank;
ears ringing, eye throbbing, you come awake
pelting down the street, gun clenched in
aching hand, Dad's blood on rosy blouse,
red on red, buttoned up to flushed neck
dorkstyle. He'd shouted *stupid little slut*
you dress like a whore because he read
your diary, but the boy you want has never
talked to you, never noticed you, never
spread his father's expensive brains
across the wall with a .44
why'd a jobless small-town surgeon
need to keep a macho hand cannon
in his desk, not safe-locked or nightstand-
handy for the stealthy midnight robber
he claimed would take your virginity,
his Callaway clubs, his Sony plasma TV,
his Rockwell prints, the Tiffany jewelry
Mom already hocked to keep family afloat
in the boring sea of bills he thought
was so below a hippocrate like him.
When he shouted you in for your exam
you remember the slide of the gun drawer
but nothing else, not 'til the pavement,
sweating, throat raw meat, stopping
in the blossoming dogwoods to shove

the gun into the front of your jeans
like some ghetto gangster on TV,
but you're a skinny schoolgirl, nerd-
pale and invisible, so you run to safety,
the dark basement of the town library,
curl under a carrel, breathe comforting book
dust, dig through your change for a shiny penny
and wish for a waking dream, a wrinkle in time.
You open your eyes: the disaster's mapped
in stark spatter over your favorite shirt,
you pull out his machine, press the cold barrel
to your honor-roll forehead and squeeze —

Part VI
Strange Corners

Uncanny Valley Girl

Mister Mori thought I'd find you eerie
with your tepid flesh and passive face.
In your assembly I see naught but beauty
sans the animal flaws of the feminine race.

Your polymer skin is smooth as bisque,
your eyes a cerulean unseen in Nature.
Swains may recoil from servo whir and whisk;
the deus of your machina's my favorite feature.

Your hardwired love is steadfast, unflinching,
though I'm a toadish sinner, obese and aging.
I smashed all my mirrors, dreading my reflection
but you swept up the shards with perky affection:

"Your credit is perfect ... no reason to worry!
Death is for losers. Let's buy your new body!"

Dime Novel

"Nothin' but a one-horse twin,"
disparages sexy Sheriff Dyslexia,
staring arrogant at the Dustbite Boys
astride their poor swaybacked pony.

At low noon, a Siamese centaur gallops down,
mythic hooves rolling with the tumbleweeds,
corded torsos backed like Janus,
arrows raised in a riot of elbows.

The Sheriff hears "raw!" instead of "draw!"
and while she scans in confusion
for sores in the absence of saddle
the hostile horsey Cupids pierce her heart.

They steal her star and hit the bar,
sling whiskey, then twinnish insults
about who's the horse's ass.
One shoots: they're both scored.

When the monster's cold, the ichor dried,
enter the janitors: the Dustbite Boys,
boots and guns shined like Sunday,
swayback pony snorting proud.

They'll hire a yellow Yankee paperman
and clean up as pulpbound heroes
instead of star-stuck survivors who simply
skipped to the end of the horse opera's libretto.

Squidliquor

Maybe my sloshing id baits my tongue
with a barbed blue joke; perhaps a party
angler trolls up the President or Pope.

Regardless, I open my mouth: a weird
fox-pawed, cock-tailed squid squeezes
past gullet and palate, lips and teeth,
and in beaky, inky calamari glory slaps
wetly on the shiny parquet floor.

Jaw clenched against further cephalopody,
I murmur clammy apologies as the bodies
ogle their vodka martinis, the ceiling, ignoring
icky stinking tentacles creeping over loafers,
up waxed legs, damply tweaking Calvin Kleins.

Our host smiles like a fish in formaldehyde,
gushes about the weather as the squid wriggles
gluey gray stains across her Sacramucca sofa.

Finally, my cocktail monster chills, wiggles nimble
feet and flees for warmer waters under the bridge.

Sofa Nervosa

The world wobbling on an axis
of apocalypse, the TV host declares
the night's top story is the horror
of a starlet who shaved her head.

Behind you, the cat begins to puke:
not just a single hork-hork-*blorf*, but
a comet of vomit, a fishstinky hairball
streak hurling from room to room

in some frantic purgatory anxiety.
You sigh, suffer mutely, stare
at the tube, pray for the weather
and ponder the razor.

Looped

— the morning light's a sharp note
sawing your staticky head in half
as if Jimmy'd strung his Strat
with catgut, cat still attached,
howling like a Nawlins hurricane
blasting the fluff from preening birds,
their bones filled with air and chirps.
Your bones feel loose, your marrow
a maraca, but they aren't song-hollow
drums – too heavy – more like long
anvils where little devils forge sin
of the most joyabolical kind.
If Lucifer used to be an angel
then a devil's heart must beat
below every feathery breast
or at least that's what Jane said
right before she told you, "Girl,
don't take no wooden horses,"
as the glittery Stoli fairy dragged
her into her own *sinfonía privado.*
Thoughts heavy as canary dust,
dancing light as dirty hobnail boots,
Goody Twoshots saves the evening;
she always bra-stashes sweaty
bills for truckstop waffles & the sweet
black hotblood of owl-life, *mas Java*
por favor, la jeva no quiero queso!
Sad that the delicious roasty ocean
can never Mozart away the Gwar
gigging your body at sunrise —

Part VII
Unshelled Evolution

Book Smarts

In our old apartment, Gary and I discovered
that stacked boxes of hardbacks are perfect
for stopping random drive-by bullets.
We soldiered on until our neighbor's parade
of night-shifty visitors and chemical stenches
seemed more dire than any broken lease. So

we shed the heavy bookworm cocoon and flew
to Tranquil Avenue. Most days, the newlyweds
across the street screamed like calicos in heat;
at night they'd roll home, arm-in-arm, wailing
whisky ballads. On Sundays, mindful of hangovers
and tired homeowners, the larksome jack next door
fired up his fatpipe hog two hours before our alarm,
lingered astride his pride, enjoying the engine's croon.

We considered cookies, an over-the-fence chat,
but glimpsed blued metal and crosshatched walnut
under his iron cross belt. Gary hated to call our realtor
a lying bitch, so after surveillance we decided our lout
was bluff, an undercover cop. Then we quietly rebuilt
our library in thick oak on the narcward side of the house.

Dumb

I remember the faux-granite café table,
your graceful hand smoothing your blue
silk batik dress as you lamented the cost
of your daughter's crow-footed tuition.

Not merely a teacher but a professor, you
knew college like a chef knows meat. Score-
happy undergrads claimed you as a favorite
while you eased them into life's grinder,
took them for treats before they left town

for rosy jobcoggery. Tenure buttered
your budget for croissants and birch beer,
but oh, your kid's crimson-lined hunger –
on a tweed skirt paycheck, Harvard's *hard.*

But it would cost her almost nothing here,
I said. Your oh-please smile marked me
naïve. You declared your only child
deserved class with *smart* people.

The pastry went to sand in my mouth.
I wanted to leap onto the brittle table, yell
Woo howdy no don't let yer purty little gal
git learnt longside fool rubes like me!

My dumb face surely flushed Hoosier red
but you chatted on about racism, social justice
as the kid at the counter carved fresh turkey
and I realized I'd never have the cash to pay
for the sandwich I wanted to feed you.

So I snuffed my reply with a bite of turnover pie
as tinsel wisdoms spilled from your unbruised lips.
Let you assume silence was assent. That I left
in mute admiration of your enlightenment.

Searching for Signs of Life in the Bottom of a Cup of Cold Coffee

The graduate students are lunching
on bitter cafeteria coffee, lardy fries
and cold roast beef, dreaming and complaining.
One is tired of literature. She wants to be a farmer,
grow radishes and onions, maybe raise a cow or two.
The other sighs, "I just can't wait to get out of here
and have a real life!"

I imagine her going to a huge supermarket
to buy her future: passing shelves of powdered reality
in dusty cardboard, steering her cart around pyramids
of shiny cans that exclaim, "New Leben Lite!
One third less angst than regular Leben!"
She heads to the gourmet section, picks out
a tastefully foiled package: "La Vita Bella.
Made from 100% meaningful existence.
Just add college and simmer for one year."

I want to ask her who she thinks has a Real Life.
Does it belong to Linda, her days crammed full
of paperwork and meetings, Starbucks runs and clocks,
head aching from a squinty PDA screen before she lies
down in a hotel bed, only to wake a few hours later
for an early morning flight, the after-imaged dreams
of kids and long-gone lovers burning behind her eyes?

Or does it belong to Betty, a housewife, her life dirty
diapers and bowls of mac and cheese, endless ironing
while her husband naps through the news? Then it's a kiss
and two minutes of sweaty blundering on a creaky mattress.
While he snores, she lies awake, imagining gorgeous
orchid wildernesses, bright jungle birds, and safaris
to all those places in the National Geographic shows.

And could it belong to Susan, a scientist in a mad rush
to kill, photograph, and bag all her tiny rainforest insects?
She wishes she could become a modern-day Noah, but
her footlocker is small and leaky; she cannot curse
the gaunt loggers and their swollen-bellied children,
but as the stink of smoke and the snarl of chainsaws
jar her awake, she prays for dry clothes,
a pantyhose job, and luxurious ignorance.

Maybe living is just a matter of respiration and perspiration:
experiences inhaled, ideas exhaled, decisions sweated out.
Maybe Shakespeare was right all along: it's acting the part
you've accepted for yourself, heartbeat never quite steady
as you manage to celebrate every scene, even as the last reel
in the camera is slowly rolling onto its cold gray spool.

A Boy's Guide to Neoteny

At the rest home, it's Pet Therapy Day
and a discharged sergeant, 40 years
old, legs lost to a roadside explosion,
holds a fuzzy month-old ginger kitten,
whispers fond nonsense and buries
his rough face in the purring fur.

Across the sea, a skinny son, barely teen, torn
from mother and hut, is given greenshirt rank
and a machete. Soldiers promise him manhood
if he'll silence the comfort girl's wailing newborn
in the barren field. Weaklings starve. So the boy
obeys, and buries his own heart beside soft bones.

Near the tiny grave, ants silently wage formic warfare,
black versus red, the chitinous adults hard-programmed
to flourish in murderous places. They coldly nurture
captured larvae. Sleeping pupae, legs folded like prayer,
dream of nectar, loyal aphids, and unshelled evolution.

Tomorrow, a boy with a glass ant farm gets a lecture
from his ginbottled father: "Grow the hell up already!"
The kid, keen observer of bug life and robot battles,
steadfast fan of Peter Pan and placid axolotls,
refuses.

Ocean

I remember the last time I felt the ocean. It was at Port Isabel, near Padre Island, the week after spring break. The beach had a hangover: crumpled beer cans and cigarette butts, candy wrappers and used condoms. Herring gulls squabbled over choice bits of trash and cried as they wheeled in the sky. The sun was sulking under a blanket of clouds. An unseasonably chilly wind, greasy with salt, blew fitfully across the waves.

The sea spread out to the horizon, rippling like a vast sheet of gray-green satin. The easy roll of the distant swells turned to a surge of foam at the shoreline. The whispering roar of the waves was calling me, pulling my blood as the moon pulls the tide.

I found a clear spot of sand and stripped down to my swimsuit. The wind knotted my skin with goosebumps. I left my sneakers on; the sand was full of hidden fish hooks.

I crossed the beach and waded in, shivering and wincing at the first cold bite of salt on my legs. The current tugged at my ankles. I'd been warned about the undertow; it had dragged under dozens of unwary swimmers. I imagined the victims being pulled down, down into the dark water to become a feast for deep-sea crabs. But today, the undertow was no watery mugger; it was insistent but gentle, almost playful, like a man pulling his lover behind a tree for a kiss. I splashed out into the waves until my toes could barely find the sandy bottom.

I felt a sudden thrill of fear as the swell lifted me as though I were a sliver of driftwood. This was no polite suburban swimming pool. This water was powerful. It wasn't just the force of sheer mass that I felt. Perhaps what I sensed was the kinetic energy of the rolling molecules, the innate force of the wet, heavy children of gases joined in explosive union. Perhaps what I felt came from chemical instinct, the miniature sea in my own veins faltering in the vastness of its ancient birthplace.

After a few minutes, the surges no longer frightened me. The rising, falling swell was the steady breathing of a sleeping creature. The rhythm lulled me, and I lay back in the water and let myself float.

I closed my eyes and let my mind drift. My thoughts left my body and spiraled up, up into the sky, through the misty sheets of clouds into outer space. I imagined I could see the earth spreading below me, nothing of human civilization visible. The sea wrapped the planet like a blue amoeba that had flattened itself around a grain of sand. The sea was moving, pulsing in slow, millennial currents around the globe.

I realized that the sea itself is alive, not just a soup of fish and salt and seaweed, but truly alive. All living things within it, from delicate crystalline plankton to hardy killer whales, are part of a vast, liquid body. The ocean's organisms eat and breed and die to be reabsorbed into the system, life and death locked in a perpetual embrace, just like the cells in my own body.

I had never seen myself as anything but an individual before, but now I realized that I, too, was a cell in the salty blood. And someday I would be gone, broken down into nitrogen and carbon and water, nothing of my essence left but a few genes in future generations of cells.

I felt myself drift away farther into outer space until the Earth looked like a fist-sized white and azure jewel hanging against the blackness. I turned my face toward the heat of the sun. It was swollen, shining the wrong color, pregnant with disaster.

Then it burst, a shell of flame and shock ripping out across space. The fire tore across the Earth, tearing off its living skin, shattering its rocky bones.

I thought I could hear the beautiful blue creature scream as it exploded into cosmic steam.

I woke with a start, shaking. I was so cold I couldn't feel my feet. My skin was white against the dark water. I swam back to shore, my arms and legs weak against the waves. I staggered onto the beach and found my towel and clothes. After I dried off and dressed, I jogged along the beach to coax the blood back into my chilled limbs.

I knew I couldn't go back into the water, but I didn't want to leave. So I spent the rest of the day searching for shells in the wet gray sand. The clouds broke in the late afternoon, and I hiked to the jetty to watch the sundown show of brilliant purples and delicate pinks and oranges.

After the horizon had faded to the blackest blue,

the real show began. The night tide was thick with phosphorescent plankton that flashed in green alarm at any disturbance. Every crashing wave sent up a spray of ghostly fireworks. Glowing sea foam oozed like lava in the crevices of the jagged black rocks.

Finally, my eyes would hardly stay open, and I started to shiver in the night breeze. I turned away from the jetty, trudged back down the road, through the dingy trailer park to a rickety beach shack in which even the plastic had rusted. I drew a tub of hot, clear, uninteresting water, poured in perfumed bubble bath as faint compensation, and washed the sea from my skin and hair.

But it could not be washed from my mind. As I lay in my bed that night, I could still feel my body rise and fall with the waves, the sensation like phantom pain from an amputated limb.

Permian Basin Blues

The sky's the color of my old blue jeans,
and the land is pulled tight by drought.
The fields wear prickly cotton crewcuts
shaved by old farmers and good ol' boys,
everything boxed in barbed-wire squares.

This town is barely a limestone roadcut,
and I'm a misplaced bit of granite or flint,
an arrow from some alien tribe lodged
mysteriously amid the bleached strata,
crystallizing under tons of archaic karst
that grind keen edges to dull gray sand.

So I'll drive out to some big, wide ranch,
strip down to the pink to let my skin breathe,
and I'll dance for pleasure, I'll dance for rain,
I'll dance for lightning, I will dance for pain,
I'll scream 'til the fossils stir deep in the earth
and rise to the surface, hard skeletal denizens
of the long-dried ocean surging up through the rock,
a tectonic to shock the town from its flatland coma.

And if the rancher drives out, armed
with a shotgun and a look of confusion,
then I will just smile at him and say
that I'm just trying to make some waves.

Photograph of a Lady, Circa 1890

There she sits still, image
locked on yellowed paper,
beautiful, but a little stiff.
She was posing in a time when
photography was serious business;
you had to be a prepared centerpiece,
not a storm petrel caught mid-second
in flight over the smooth, rolling waves.

Her clothes and parasol
are the fine white of sea salt,
but her dress is soft linen armor;
that delicate skin never felt the burn
of the hot sun and she never ran through
the seaspray and the crashing waves, so cold
they seem electric in their force and shock.

No, the rough ocean was the realm of whalers
and half-naked heathen islanders, not ladies.
So she spent summertime trips to the beach
under a wide umbrella and drank mint tea,
and the vast green sea rolled on without her.

The smooth line of her jaw is fuzzy;
did the photographer's hand tremble
as he slowly exposed her image,
or was it a problem in the solution
sloshing in small waves in the pan
in his landlocked darkroom?

Her body is gone, only this
flat, crackling image remains,
but even now, still she trembles
deep in the paper, where particles
that form her likeness waltz
in quick, subatomic union.

Perhaps more of her still moves
in the scattered elements her soul shed:
she's in the ground, she's in the air,
and as her blood once thrilled
at hearing exotic tales of travel
to places that she could never see,
now she travels in a slow, millennial
circulation around the continents,
pulled by the sun and moon, and now
she knows what Ocean really means.

About the Author

Lucy A. Snyder is the author of the forthcoming Del Rey novel *Spellbent* and the short story collections *Sparks and Shadows* and *Installing Linux on a Dead Badger*. Her poetry has appeared in *Full Unit Hookup, Strange Horizons, Chiaroscuro, Snow Monkey, Lady Churchill's Rosebud Wristlet,* and *Greatest Uncommon Denominator*. She also served as a poetry editor for *HMS Beagle*.

Lucy was born in South Carolina but grew up in the cowboys-and-cactus part of Texas. She currently lives in Worthington, Ohio with a pack of cats and her husband/occasional co-author Gary A. Braunbeck.

You can learn more about her at:

www.lucysnyder.com

About the Cover Artist

Ursula Vernon is probably best known as the creator of the webcomics *Digger* and *Nurk*. She is also the author of *It Made Sense At The Time*, a book of her selected sketches. Vernon is the daughter of an artist, but didn't begin drawing until she was 17. Much of her art is digital, but she also uses combinations of acrylic ink, fluid acrylic, watercolor, gouache, and colored pencil. She currently lives in North Carolina with cats and far too many art supplies.

You can find more of her artwork at:

www.metalandmagic.com

Acknowledgements

Thanks to Natalie Shapero and Christopher Conlon for their revision suggestions. Thanks also to the editors of the magazines who first published some of the pieces in this collection:

- "Modernism" – *Snow Monkey,* Ravenna Press, Seattle, Spring 2002.
- "Subtlety" – *Greatest Uncommon Denominator Magazine,* Spring 2008.
- "Sympathy" – *Strange Horizons,* November 2006.
- "Trepanation" – *Strange Horizons,* July 2006.
- "The Fish and the Bicycle" – *Sparks and Shadows*, HW Press, May 2007.
- "glowfish" – *Sparks and Shadows*, HW Press, May 2007.
- "Babel's Children" – *Star*Line,* May 2008.
- "The Monster Between The Sparks" (published as "Dark Matter") – *Chiaroscuro,* January 2002.
- "Flyboy" – *Strange Horizons,* April 30, 2007.
- "Crete, Kentucky: Passie Fay's Lament" – *Full Unit Hookup Magazine,* 2008.
- "Uncanny Valley Girl" – *Raven Electrick,* November 30, 2007.
- "Searching For Signs of Life In the Bottom of a Cup of Cold Coffee" (previously titled "Real Life") – *Full Unit Hookup Magazine,* Spring 2002.
- "Ocean" – *Lady Churchill's Rosebud Wristlet,* Issue #6, May 2000.
- "Permian Basin Blues" *Lady Churchill's Rosebud Wristlet,* Issue #7, October 2000.
- "Photograph of a Lady, Circa 1890" – *Lady Churchill's Rosebud Wristlet,* Issue #7, October 2000.

www.ingramcontent.com/pod-product-compliance
Ingram Content Group UK Ltd.
Pitfield, Milton Keynes, MK11 3LW, UK
UKHW020223250726
13967UKWH00001B/164

9 781894 953559